everything
i wish i knew

at seventeen

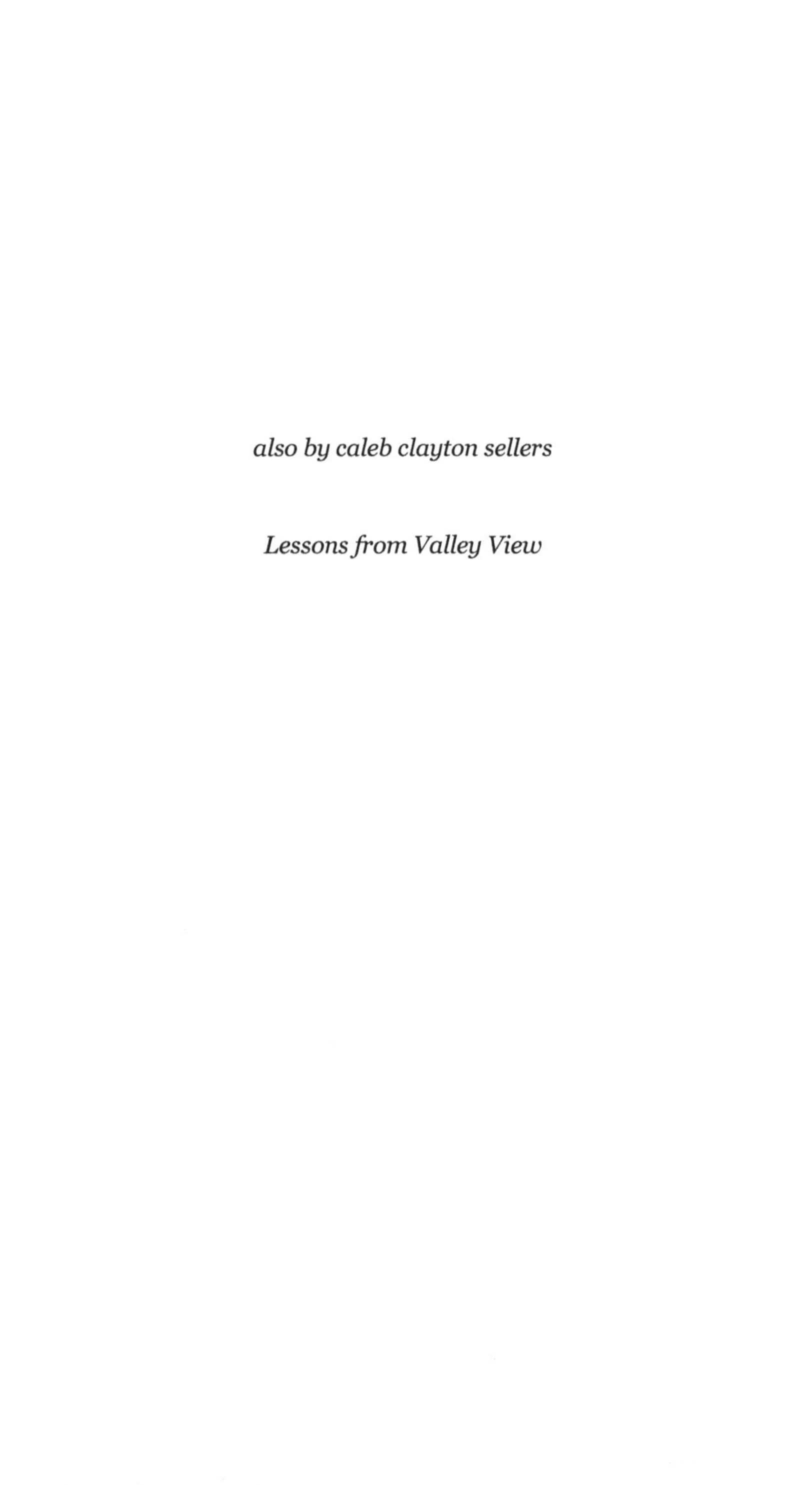

also by caleb clayton sellers

Lessons from Valley View

everything
i wish i knew
at seventeen

caleb clayton sellers

Rural Renaissance
Publishing

Rural Renaissance Publishing
Bonifay, Florida

ISBN: 979-8-234-06411-0

First Edition, 2026

Cover, design, and illustrations by Caleb Clayton Sellers

Author photo by Paulk's Media Productions

For permissions, inquiries, or information regarding bulk orders, signed copies, classroom use, bookstore partnerships, or author visit, please contact the author through email: calebclaytonsellers@gmail.com

to those who challenged me the most

while loving me even more

—	*my students*

thank you

for your words

in *milk and honey*, it

was the first poetry book i

ever read when i was seventeen

and it's a source of inspiration

i keep coming back to

—   *to rupi kaur*

note from the author

after self-publishing *lessons from valley view*, i genuinely thought i would put an end to my self-publishing journey. a lot of these poems were going to be in a third chapter of *lessons*; however, i ultimately decided that the book should solely focus on the original collection—and i'm glad i stuck with that decision.

for the majority of the past year, i had been writing, editing, and submitting my forthcoming poetry manuscript in an attempt get it traditionally published—in hopes that it would be the best chance for my work to be in the hands of many readers—however, i've quickly learned that publishing is not what i thought it was, so instead of waiting for someone else to give me a chance, i decided to give myself a chance and create another self-published book on a whim.

i looked through those poems i discarded, and i

noticed how they all appeared as words of wisdom

from my experience of moving back home after

college to begin my career in teaching at the very same

school i never wanted to come back to.

aside from learning how to teach, i've also learned

how to heal many of the wounds i had from the

hometown i ran away from, and as i close this final

chapter to my time as a high school teacher for my

hometown, i thought it was the perfect time to release

a book of everything i have learned since the last time

i was here—*at seventeen.*

i am writing this book in hopes that any young adult

can learn the lessons i believed to be most impactful

for me at this stage in life. and for my students, this is

so you can learn something from me once more.

everything
i wish i knew
about hurting

i'm turning my pain into

after a long day at school

you come and see me

after spending all day with him

you come and see me

when your wife is at work

you come and see me

after you party all night

you come and see me

after hanging with your friends

you come and see me

after putting your children to sleep

you come and see me

after seeing all of you

i can't see myself

for i am no longer breathing

— *a breath of fresh air*

why do i have to be caught

in the middle of this

nothing is the way i wanted

i don't want to be spiteful

and mean and resentful

but that is my default

to family issues

i will never get pass

i can't fix it right away

it takes time

and time annoys me

my family has stressed me out

for so long

now i'm trying to move into adulthood

but i'm surrounded by the pain

i had during childhood

—   *i am so confused*

how do i heal

let go

grow

move on

without being distant

i don't understand

and i want to be hopeful

but my mind prevents that

i am afraid

of becoming a father

i fear i will hurt him

and i will live to regret it

for the rest of my life

—   *generational trauma*

is this fantasy

only to live

within the walls

of my mind

or can it be achieved

in my reality

—   *why am i never satisfied*

i've only seen sleepovers on tv

where the friends stay up late

watching movies they shouldn't

laughing until the parents wake up

and tell them all to go to bed

— *i never had one*

breakfast in the morning

before our big day

friends around the table

like it's the last supper

and you're my Jesus

—　*pancakes & prayer*

is this light liquid

the source of my happiness

or is it simply the key to the doors

my mind has kept shut from my soul

i am ashamed to enjoy the taste

but i yearn the effect it has on me

for this state of blurriness

allows me to see clearly

is addiction upon my horizon

or is moderation the new way

to live a life of peace and tranquility

in one's gifts

my stomach is baptized

in bright white bliss

and my mind is opened

to joy and risk

your insecurities will make you say

"this whole time

i've lied to myself

to believe that i am more attractive

than what i really am

everything makes so much sense

i'm so unattractive

which is the reasoning

for how guys interact with me

my people are other medium ugly losers

if i want to make it in this world

i have to work for the appearance

that is acceptable to reality"

— *you are beautiful inside and out*

i lust after

a version of myself

that does not exist

i don't take care

of my body and health

because i'm not confident in that area

i do take care of my mind and heart

because i'm confident in those

i'm too hard on myself

i constantly let myself down

before i even start

telling myself i can't

when i've already done it before

what is this

constantly contradicting myself

and every decision

i attempt to create so many ideas

and yet none are complete

i feel like wasted potential

so bright

but the light never shines

flickering

but it's a brand new bulb

the devil will tell you

"you're not all that

you're still unattractive

and one you like loves you

you'll have to settle

for lustful hookups

and terrible men

you are not allowed to feel

you will lose everything

you worked so hard for

and never recover

emotionally"

—   *you are blessed and highly favored*

snow falls from the floridian sky

and i'm left feeling puzzled

every snowflake feels like a trap

to fall into as if i have no choice

but to let it hit my cheek

from the wind i need to face

the weatherman lies

and he sits upon his throne

casting stones

to those below

we're the ones freezing

and he's throwing asbestos onto set

i'm the farm girl

deceived from those put in place

to help the poor

—   *we're not in kansas anymore*

i wish i never knew

the truths you were hiding

from me

—   *those who can't face reality*

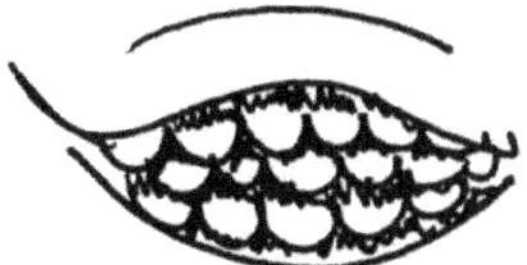 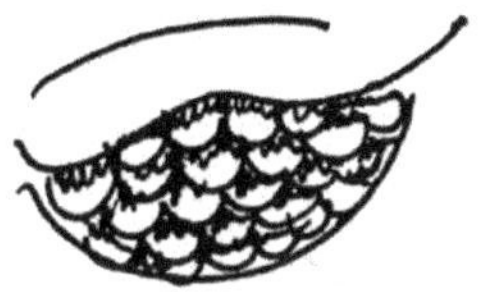

you walk through this world

with your eyes closed

because you're comfortable

in the darkness

— *you hide the truth from yourself*

you have your hand on the switch

but you can't find the confidence

to flip it

it's okay

but there is nothing to be afraid of

you know that when you do it

the light will shine

—   *what's stopping you*

sexy brain

magnetic personality

incredible taste

beautiful face

amazing body

— *i want my body to match my mind*

i want to live freely

and make nothing

but right and productive decisions

throughout my day

but i must rely on routine to function

is it scaffolding

or is it restriction

do they coexist

or am i not aligned

with what is figured out

for me

in the midst of all the positivity

i have felt in the past two weeks

i can't help but to still have a sour taste

in my heart for my lack of freedom

and companionship

the question is never

whether i have friends or not

and it is also never to assume

they don't love me

for i am highly aware of the love

and support i have from my friends

however

i always find myself feeling angry

and succumbing to delusion

when i see my friends

experiencing fun and freedom

when i am left in my mother's home

broke

and i can't seem but to feel

a sense of jealousy

when i'm not invited

or desired for separate plans

i have always hated

fighting for quality time

but i believe i've reached

the threshold of tolerance

this leads me to wonder

whether my shroud of loneliness

can be cured by a relationship

am i ready

for that kind of commitment

am i even able to open up

and allow myself

to pursue an intimate and fruitful

relationship

without feeling

lost

burdened

stressed

or scared

i've felt alone for so long

but i'm worried

that i'm still not ready

i've done so much growing

but if i fall into my old ways

i'm scared that i didn't grow at all

and i will be sent away

with no lover comforting me

only myself

as i have been

diligently

it's miraculous

how even when life

is the best it's been

i never find the time to celebrate

— *confetti*

your ego will make you say

"i want to live in my own world

only i understand myself

and i am tired of feeling shame

and embarrassment

from people

that aren't on my wavelength"

—   *they need you the most*

although i love my job

and i enjoy the tasks and responsibilities

i do not stand

for the lack of compensation and time

available to truly perform effectively

without immense amounts of sacrifice

my health and well-being

fall short every week

and i continue to find myself

struggling to be at my best

for my students

my patience is running thin

and the little things about my job

are causing me to enjoy it

less and less

i am here to teach students

about literature and writing

not to force them to adhere

to a bunch of outdated rules

taking away from my valuable time

to teach then the subject

i went to college for

— *i can't wait to get my masters
and teach at a university*

if there was an evaluation

on touching the lives of your students

building lasting relationships

listening to their issues

giving them grace

providing them supplies

supporting their dreams

inspiring them outside of the classroom

being a role model

then i'd be highly effective

— *every fuckin year*

don't use grace's name in vain

to disguise your fears

doubt

and laziness

— *you can be your dream self now*

what's the point of staying

if you're not happy

where you're at

— *there's more out there for you*

everything
i wish i knew
about healing

i'm learning

to be happy

to be proud

to be confident

to be bold

to be fearless

to heal

an ego is saddening to witness

and dangerous to experience

but damn if confidence

isn't the best bliss there is

my life is better

how i imagine it

not from the response

(or the lack thereof)

but from what i bring to the table

it's not about *what* you look at

it's about *how* you look at it

—   *it's all about your perspective*

the same way

your parents have to let go of you

you have to let go of them

—   *they don't tell you that*

boundaries

in healing

are mandatory

separation

out of shame

is forbidden

resentment

is just a way for you

to never find peace

with the people

that did their best

to raise you

— *give your parents some grace*

the perfect melody

blissfully carries me

through time and space

the complex chords

fill my heart

with a warm and deep sensation

and the cascading run

enlightens my soul

and trickles in my mind

the harmonies

make me float

and ascend into another realm

away from the stress and anxieties

and into the world of the album

when confusion and doubt

take me hostage

music alleviates my suffering

though i am forced to live this life

i've learned how to escape

into a spacious void

of warmth from the stars

forgetting my existence

being present

no longer thinking

of what i'm thinking

how i'm thinking

and why i'm thinking

of what i'm thinking

my purest form

exists in the clothing of harmonies

crowned with sparkling instrumentation

lifted on the pedestal of production

as i'm moved by the artist

and their vulnerable confessions

the renaissance

is a movement for me

to transcend into this world

and flourish as the artist

i am destined to be

today marks a new beginning

the false dawn has set

and an eternal sunshine

has lit up the future for me

the missing key is found

and my priorities of self

health

opportunity

and work

with love and passion

now rests in God's hands

i am becoming a new man

and i am so proud of myself

for clearing a path

and not getting in my way

— *less is more*

i trust my gut feeling

that radiates throughout my body

a perfect vibration

peace

this high

is what we chase

to be happy

this level of awareness

eases me with peace of knowledge

—   *there's healing in knowing*

it's time to grow up

and be more serious

and sophisticated

and learn how to live

a healthy productive life

one that benefits the world

before benefiting you

work on yourself

use your muscles

push past your limits

become accustomed

to a productive

daily routine

and a healthy lifestyle

trees in a sky

all of their own

leaves wave to me

as i sit below

we'll never meet

for you will soon knew

you will soon reap

what you've always sown

—   *the wilderness*

the swelling of intensity

rises

as i hold my breath

for what's to come

everything
i wish i knew
about living

you have so much

to be grateful for

and so much

to enjoy

in this life

you will only become

as successful

as your body

so your dreams

are only possible

through you

all of you

your vessel

will get you there

not your brain alone

it takes time

but more

importantly

effort

discipline

is self-respect

it is not

a punishment

or a lack

of freedom

don't allow

your vessel

to be a prison

to your soul

—   *exercise enlightens you*

confidence

is not the absence

of insecurities

—   *it's moving forward with your flaws*

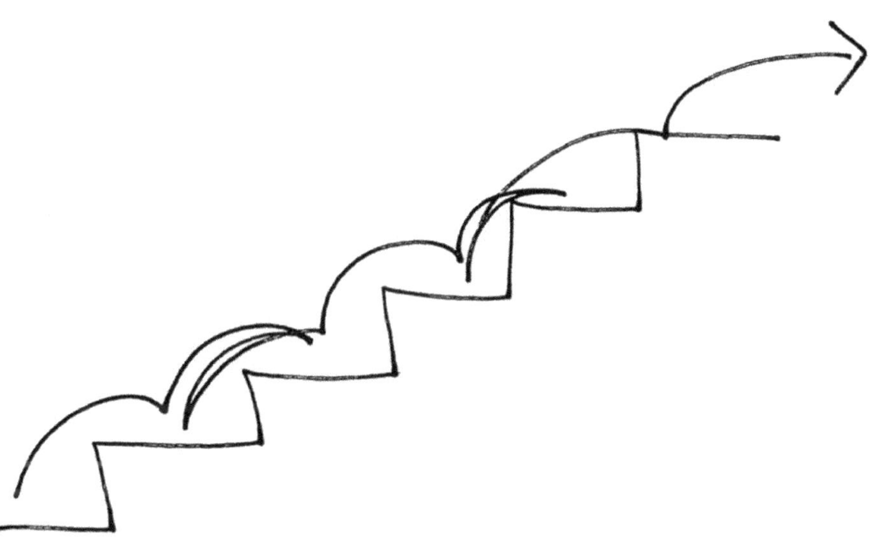

the only way

you can grow

to be the fullest

of your potential

is to prioritize

your health

and well-being

all you have to do

is be the best

version of yourself

—   *everything is making its way to you*

there is beauty in the universe

created from the cosmic crash

of feelings

from hurt experiences

every phase

and era

is beautiful

because we allowed ourselves

to enjoy our life

and exist

within the forefront

of the world

by living out loud

it's okay to feel

this fuels the growth you yearn for

allow it

trust it

feel it

more

you'll shed your skin

more times than you can count

you'll have layers

in your closet

next to the skeletons

that never see the light of the day

—   *embrace your past selves*

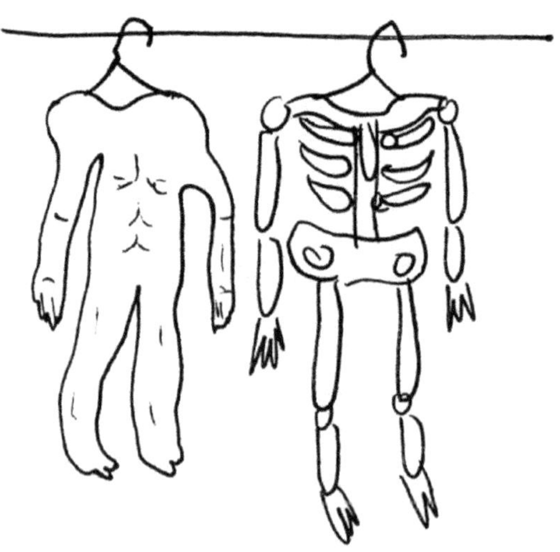

you have to

embrace your past

in order to

accept your future

life is meant

to be enjoyed

not pushed through

you can enjoy life

you don't have to

work yourself to death

making money quickly

is not important

—   *the purpose is to spread love to all*

your path

of dreams

growth

and goals

is all unique

to you

comparing your life

adds nothing

to your experience

it only makes it feel

irrelevant

it is not

—   *your life is unique so share it*

it is time

that you wake up

share your story

with the world

you've lived enough lives

for a lifetime

but no one knows

the wisdom you carry

it doesn't matter

where you come from

or what you don't have

you are worthy

of love

peace

and passion

create

do something new

chase your dreams

and never look back

wishing you did more

with your life

— *be a creator, not a consumer*

your art

and ideas

must exist

outside

your mind

—   *respect yourself by seeing it through*

i wish everyone

in my hometown

could see the world

the way i do

—   *don't be afraid to tell the truth*

you should create art

that tells everyone

about your perspective

and beliefs

so you can be an influence

— *for your hometown, first*

you'll settle for radio towers

instead of seeing paris, france

cause you believe

there's something to be afraid of

when its not what you're used to

—   *you need to see the world*

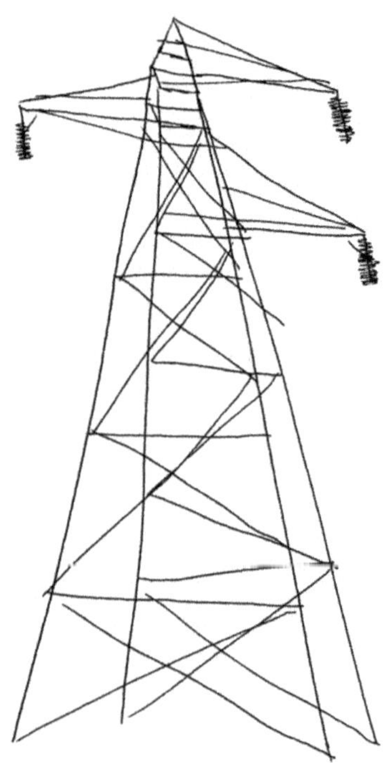

doing anything we desire

just because

is the reason

we enjoy our life

shame

embarrassment

insecurities

survivor's guilt

and fear

keep us little

you must lead

by your ability

to receive

you are an

anomaly

so show yourself

some grace

God protects me

and my intuition

is Him telling me

to move

God has given me the tools

to accomplish the task

i just have to do it

fearlessly

— *live in faith, not fear*

the lines

may be

small

but the

message is

big

—   *poetry allows*
     my soul to speak

if i stayed

i would have lost myself

—   *i needed to shine*

some days you may annoy me

and some days we may fight

but no matter the hour

my love for you was right

you deserve to be seen

to be heard and be loved

so i showed you the grace

from our Father above

one day you'll look back

and see what i've done

as a blessing or gift

cause i saw you're someone

—   *you are much more than this town*

everything
i wish i knew

about love

to gabriel,

the love of my life,

this chapter exists because of you

—   *my guardian angel*

the truth

will set

you free

—   *john 8: 31-32*

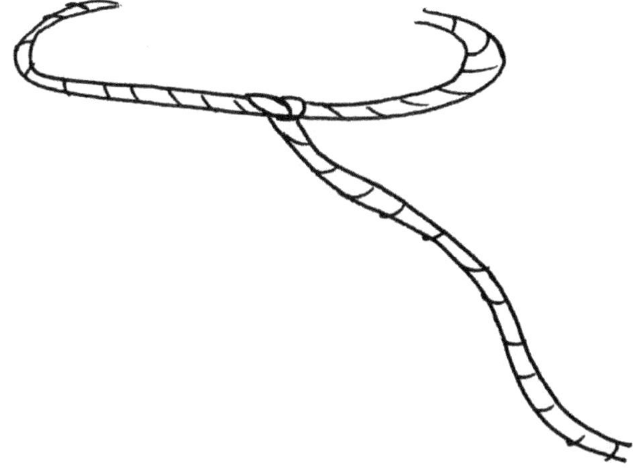

whispers of scripture

seep through the cracks

of the church

and i find myself running back

to the man who was always there

— *His love is unconditional*

He chastises the ones He loves

because if He did not

then we would be

bastards

appearance

personality

confidence

intelligence

wisdom

LOVE

empathy

sensitivity

emotion

insecurity

fear

— *we all have layers*

the relationship

with your mother

is the most inspiring

gen x

we see your triumphs

and we see your struggle

your fears are valid

and your pain is true

but it does not

define you

we love you

and want you to have the love

that you have given us

it's hard to have trust

but we are not your enemy

for we are from you

we are here

because of you

what is deep inside

can be found

what is holding you back

can be broken

what is searching for you

can be accepted

trust us and listen

for we have the answers

— *for your sacrifice and support*

the offspring are fruit

that are born to heal

what their parents

could not

do i love you

or do i love

how i remember you

—   *you were not like this before*

you're the water

i've been needing

and the garden

i've been waiting for

i could never love me

as much as you do

—   *i'm learning to receive*

your green eyes

of the earth

always ground me

in a high

where every time

you laugh

it's the thunder

in the sky

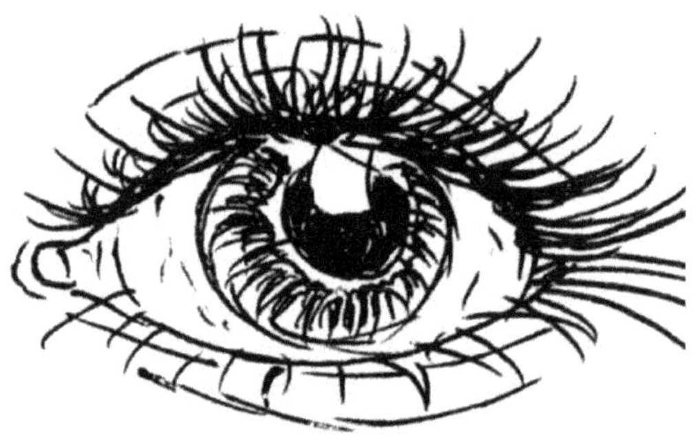

i want to create

a whole nother language

just to tell you

how much you are loved

—   *poetry is not enough*

your neck

is my favorite place to be

but learning

how to love you

is my favorite part

my pillow holds your scent

the same way you wrap your arms

around me in the morning

when it's time for you to leave

— *can't let go*

i

met

you

as your teacher but i know

you

as

my

bro

ther

it's all about relationships

— *teaching*

The Golden Rule

i never thought the day would come

when i teach my little sister

lord knows i've done it for years

but i guess it was time

to be there for her

when i was finally ready

i remember crying to my boyfriend

wishing she never experienced

what she went through when i left

but i had to leave

it's hard to think about

but i came back

and now we're closer than ever before

—   *though she will never admit it*
     i know she loves me

you already are

who you're trying

to become

—   *embrace your innermost self*

heal the world

for we have the gifts

— *gen z's mission*

acknowledgements

thank you giving me this beautiful life to write about. i
am everything because of You, and i am a witness to
the power of Your doing.

—   *my Lord and Savior*

thank you for the endless love you show me every day.
i never would have thought that i would find my
soulmate while living here. i would be nothing without
you.

—   *my love*

thank you for the twenty-four years of prayer and
protection on my life. i am honored to know that i
inspire you, and i will always love and appreciate
everything you've done for me.

—   *my family*

thank you for being my biggest supporters. i am so

blessed to have you by my side as i embark on this

journey.

— *my friends*

thank you for the many memories—all good and bad.

without you, i would not have been so inspired to find

my voice.

— *my hometown*

thank you for supporting me along this journey and

always encouraging me to stay true to myself.

— *my teachers*

thank you for being my first *fans*. i'm blessed to know

that you are all watching me follow my dreams. i will

always believe in you. i love you all.

— *my students*

about the author

Caleb Clayton Sellers is an artist, poet, and educator from the Florida Panhandle.

His work explores his life as a gay man raised in the rural South. Writing within his tradition of Southern Gothic Romanticism, his work confronts the dark and heavy inheritances of Southern life and evangelical Christianity, while ultimately turning towards healing and hope.

He is currently self-publishing his books under his imprint Rural Renaissance Publishing. His first book is *Lessons from Valley View*—an intimate poetry collection about his late grandfather's life and legacy.

You can connect with Caleb on all social media platforms *@calebclaytonsellers*. Discover more to read on Instagram *@ruralrenaissance_publishing*.

Photo by Paulk's Media Productions

about the book

everything i wish i knew at seventeen

is a poetry collection

about navigating childhood wounds

insecurities

reconciliation

and the battle between

faith and fear

this collection

offers a voice

to the hard truths

we struggle to face

serving as a kind of scripture

for those still learning

how to heal

live

and love